Alpin[es]
the Easy Way

A Wisley Handbook

Alpines the Easy Way

JOE ELLIOTT

Cassell

The Royal Horticultural Society

THE ROYAL HORTICULTURAL SOCIETY

Cassell Educational Limited
Villiers House, 41/47 Strand
London WC2N 5JE
for the Royal Horticultural Society

First published 1987
Reprinted 1988
Second edition 1991

British Library Cataloguing in Publication Data
Elliott, Joe
  Alpines the easy way. — (A Wisley handbook)
  1. Alpine garden plants
  I. Title   II. Royal Horticultural Society
  635.9′672   SB421

  ISBN 0-304-32007-2

Photographs by Joe Elliott, Harry Smith Collection
and Michael Warren
Typeset by Chapterhouse Ltd, Formby
Printed in Hong Kong by Wing King Tong Co. Ltd.

Cover: *Pulsatilla alpina* subsp. *apiifolia* (*P.a.* subsp.
sulphurea) is a native of European mountains.
Back cover: *Ramonda myconi*, a useful shade-loving alpine.
p. 1: *Penstemon hirsutus* 'Pygmaeus' is suitable for a trough.
  Photographs by Joe Elliott
p. 2: a trough planted with alpines displays a variety of
shapes and forms.
  Photograph by Harry Smith Collection

Contents

		page
Introduction		7
Raised beds		9
Island beds		9
Materials		9
Wall beds		12
Soil		12
Rock outcrops		15
Planting		15
Feeding		16
A selection of plants		17
Sinks and troughs		33
Glazed sinks		33
Simulated troughs		35
Siting and support		35
Soil and rocks		37
Planting		38
Watering and feeding		40
A selection of plants		42
The alpine house		47
Ventilation		48
Shading		48
Soil		48
Benching		49
Watering		50
Feeding		50
Cold frames		51
A selection of plants		52
Propagation		57
Seed		57
Cuttings		57
Division		59
Pests and diseases		60
Further reading		63

Introduction

While large rock gardens are almost a thing of the past these days, and even smaller ones seem to be decreasing in number, it is perhaps curious that more and more people are becoming addicted to growing the plants loosely known as 'alpines'. Witness the ever increasing membership of both the Alpine Garden Society and the Scottish Rock Garden Club.

It is not difficult to see why. The variety of forms, colours, cultural requirements and times of flowering contributed by alpines is so great that each season brings new and interesting delights. The term alpines covers a wide range of plants, many of which are not true alpines in the sense that they grow wild in the mountainous regions of the world. A creeping or carpeting habit, dwarf stature and resistance to cold are more likely characteristics of the plants broadly defined as alpines. There can hardly be a family or genus in the botanical spectrum which is not represented somewhere under the heading, which should help to dispel the old myth that they bring colour to the garden only in spring. With a little planning or good advice, alpines can give you colour and interest for virtually twelve months of the year. Nor are they plants only for the specialist. There are an enormous number of perfectly easy, reliable and very beautiful alpines, which the most complete novice can grow with no more knowledge or skill than is needed to sow a row of beans. There are, of course, many alpines which are more difficult or wayward and which, like some children, require coaxing. But that is one of the fascinations of this group of plants: the easy ones lead you on by stages to attempt some of the less predictable ones as you ascend the alpine ladder.

This book is aimed primarily at gardeners who are just starting to grow alpines for the first time. The plant lists in each section consist largely of easily available plants, which need only the most basic conditions of a sunny position in a well drained soil. But it is not my intention to exclude all those plants which may demand rather more care for, as experience is gained over the years, the grower of alpines will inevitably want to extend his or her horizons. Where special treatment is called for, it is specified in the plant lists.

Opposite: 'Citrinum', a cultivar with primrose-yellow flowers of the familiar *Alyssum saxatile* (see p. 17)

Troughs standing on cobblestones, framed by raised beds under the walls

If you have exactly the right site for a rock garden, by all means build one. It is the logical environment in which to grow alpine plants. But good rock is expensive, it takes some skill to lay correctly and, unless you are blessed with a naturally sloping site, it can look an awkward feature in the garden. For the purpose of this book, therefore, I shall disregard the rock garden proper and concentrate on three alternative types of home for growing your alpines – raised beds; sinks and troughs; and pots in an unheated greenhouse or alpine house.

Raised beds

Being semi-formal, a raised bed is a much easier feature to fit into a garden scheme than a rock garden. It can be built to almost any size and shape – rectangular, round, oval, L-shaped, or whatever form suits your particular circumstances. The site should be in the open, well away from the drips of trees and from the constant shadow of trees or buildings.

MATERIALS

There is a wide choice of materials for building the retaining walls of the bed. The obvious one is walling stone, constructed dry, that is without cement, so that plants can be encouraged to grow in the narrow cracks between the stones. It is best to start by digging a narrow trench, a few inches deep and about a foot (30 cm) wide, and to lay some of the larger flat stones close together in this to act as a mini-foundation for the walls. It is not going to carry a very heavy load, so concrete foundations are unnecessary. On top of this, build up your stones layer by layer, sloping the wall slightly inwards as it rises and, if possible, sloping each piece of stone inwards (see figure 1, p. 11). This will allow rain to soak back into the bed, rather than running outwards where it might wash away the soil or even the plants growing in the wall face. A height of about 18 to 20 inches (45–40 cm) is adequate; less than a foot (30 cm) and the bed will lack impact. It is better to make the bed no more than 5 to 6 feet (1.5–1.8 m) wide or there may be difficulty in weeding and tending the plants. When laying the stones, be sure to 'bond' them; that is to say, avoid placing the vertical edge of a stone directly in line with the edge of the stone below it. Two vertical cracks, one above the other, will always be a weak spot. Also, try to choose large stones to form the corners (see figure 2, p. 11).

Alternative materials for the walls are wooden railway sleepers: bricks, preferably old weathered ones; or even concrete building blocks. None look as attractive as walling stone, but they serve the same purpose of raising your alpine bed above the surrounding ground.

With bricks or concrete blocks, cement will have to be used, although it need not be a very strong mixture. One part of cement

Raised beds built of Cotswold walling stone

to six of builders' sand should hold the structure intact. And the walls will have to be built upright, and not sloping inwards.

Railway sleepers are laid on their sides and, if the bed is to be more than one sleeper high, must be fixed together to stop them moving sideways (see figure 3). Some builders' merchants supply substantial metal staples, which should be galvanized for preference, and these can be driven into the sleepers with a heavy hammer, the staple spanning the joints and holding them together. Otherwise, you can buy some of the heaviest gauge of galvanized wire, cut it into 6-inch (15 cm) lengths and then turn about 2 inches (5 cm) of each end of the pieces at right angles. If you are reduced to this method of securing the sleepers, it may be easier to drill holes at the appropriate distances in the wood to take the angled ends of the home-made staples. Use a drill one gauge smaller than your wire to ensure a good hold.

There is a fifth material suitable for building raised beds – the peat blocks which are cut as fuel and which give off such a delicious scent when burnt. They are not very stable, however, and tend to disintegrate over the years. They are mostly used by alpine specialists for some of their more esoteric peat-loving plants, so are perhaps a little beyond the brief of this book. But keep them in mind as your enthusiasm grows. (For further information, see the Wisley handbook, *The Peat Garden*, by Alfred Evans.)

10

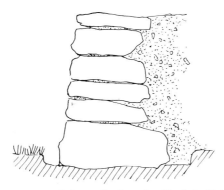

Figure 1:   cross-section of the wall of a raised bed, built to slope slightly inwards

Figure 2:   a raised bed with the stones correctly 'bonded' and a large stone at the corner

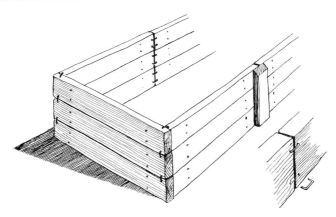

Figure 3:   constructing a raised bed with railway sleepers

11

WALL BEDS

So far we have considered only the island bed. A raised bed may also be constructed against the wall of a building or incorporated in the top of the wall of a terrace, using one of the materials already mentioned.

Obviously, the wall of your house is no place for such a bed; inevitably, it would result in moist soil above the damp course, defeating the purpose of that essential part of the house. But the wall of an outbuilding without a damp course, where a small amount of rising damp would do no harm, or better still a stone or brick dividing wall in your garden, can make an excellent site for a raised bed. One of the limiting factors of a wall bed is that it will have only one aspect. A north-facing bed will be the most difficult to fill, though there are some shade-loving alpines, including many of the primulas, *Sanguinaria canadensis*, *Hacquetia epipactis*, *Anemone nemorosa* in its numerous forms, and others. Semi-shade lovers, for example, *Chiastophyllum oppositifolium*, *Cyclamen hederifolium* and *Phlox* 'Chattahoochee', can go into an east bed. Most alpines will tolerate a west aspect and all the rest can be planted in a south-facer. Another slight disadvantage is that some of the taller plants will tend to grow away from the restricted light on the wall side and lean at an angle.

For an alpine bed combined with a terrace wall, it is best to build the wall of the terrace a foot (30 cm) or so higher than the level of the lawn or the paving which it retains. Then build another wall on the upper level about a foot (30 cm) high, so that you are left with a trough to be filled with soil.

SOIL

The one characteristic which nearly all alpine plants have in common is a love of good drainage. Few will enjoy life in a heavy clay soil. The choice of soil for a raised bed is therefore important. Something approximating to John Innes potting compost No. 2, with some extra grit added, should be the aim, though to fill a sizable bed with bought-in JI compost would leave a sizable hole in your pocket.

The alternative is to mix your own soil, which should consist of good loam, moss peat and coarse grit in equal parts by volume. If

Opposite: the shade-loving *Ramonda myconi*, above, in a north-facing crevice of a raised bed (see p. 29)

Phlox 'Chattahoochee', below, prefers a slightly shady position (see p. 26)

the loam can be from turf stacked for a year or so, then broken down and put through a $\frac{1}{2}$-inch (1 cm) sieve, so much the better. Failing that, top soil skimmed from the border or kitchen garden will serve, provided it is in good heart and not too heavy. If your soil is naturally limy, which the majority of alpines prefer, you can use any form of grit or stone chippings. The $\frac{1}{2}$ to $\frac{3}{4}$-inch (1–2 cm) grade is about right, though a few larger pieces will do no harm. The most readily available is usually pea gravel, that is, gravel washed and graded to an average size of a fairly hearty garden pea. However, if you live on acid soil and intend to grow ericaceous and other lime-hating plants, such as Gentiana sino-ornata, the grit must be of granite or sandstone. Remember that, when you mix your own soil, you may have to spend some time removing weeds, particularly in the first year. Ready-made John Innes compost is, or should be, sterilized and weed-free.

It is a good plan to mix at least some of the soil before constructing the raised bed, especially if walling stone is being used. The soil (or compost) can then be packed into the spaces between and behind the stones to ensure that no air pockets are left. It will also help to level up any stones with irregular sides or of uneven thickness.

When filling in the main body of soil, it is important to firm it well, otherwise it will consolidate over the months and sink below the top of the retaining walls, which looks unsightly. Spread the soil a few inches deep over the whole area of the bed and go all over it with a tamper or your two feet; follow this with another few inches of soil, press it down and repeat the process until the bed is full. As long as the soil is sufficiently gritty, the vital drainage will not be impeded.

Before building the bed, it is sensible also to have a few plants at hand which will enjoy clothing the vertical walls. It is far easier to plant them as you build than to try pushing them in from the front when the wall is complete. Sun-loving plants like silver saxifrages, aethionemas and some of the campanulas are suitable and, on the shadier east and north walls, ramondas, certain primulas and dwarf ferns.

When the wall is a foot (30 cm) or so high, you can start to insert the plants. To do this, remove the plant from its pot, squeeze the root ball slightly and place it beside the vertical edge of a stone. Lay the next stone in line and press it firmly against the other side of the root ball, leaving as narrow a gap as possible. Once the layer above has been built, the plant will be held securely in position. Make sure there are no air pockets around the roots so that the plant is encouraged to root back into the body of the bed.

Like other aethionemas, 'Warley Rose' does best in full sun (see p. 17)

ROCK OUTCROPS

With the walls built and all the soil in place, your raised bed will look pretty stark. This will cure itself in a year or two, when the plants of differing heights and forms have grown. But you can hasten the process of furnishing the bed by incorporating one or two small outcrops of rock and, at the same time, provide some inch-wide crevices for those alpines which like to seek out the moist coolness found in such places, for instance, saxifrages, *Omphalodes luciliae* and *Potentilla nitida*.

PLANTING

After the hard slog of the building operations, the temptation may well be to rush out to the nearest nursery and buy enough plants to fill the whole bed. This would be a mistake. The wiser course is to go to a nursery in March or April and acquire a few plants which you like in flower, then to pay monthly visits, choosing several plants each time, until the bed is complete. This way, the flowering times should be well spread over the year. The fact that the plants are in flower when they are bought is of no consequence; they will all be pot-grown and can be planted without disturbance to the roots. Just be careful not to let them dry out for the

15

Androsace lanuginosa, one of the most popular members of an extensive genus

first few weeks. Remember, too, that most alpines bloom for a relatively short period and try to vary the interest by selecting different leaf forms and growth habits – for instance, mingling upright growers and bun-shaped plants with creepers and trailers.

It is difficult to give average planting distances for such a diverse group of plants as alpines. However, in the absence of any other information, a safe compromise would be to put a plant 6 to 8 inches (15–20 cm) from its nearest neighbour. If any individual plant proves too vigorous, it can usually be moved after a year or so, taking care to keep as much soil as possible round the roots.

FEEDING

As a group, alpines are not greedy feeders and few would appreciate farmyard manure in their diet; nor would they take kindly to a dose of general garden fertilizer. They do, however, need some sustenance of a more gentle nature to keep them growing and flowering. Probably the safest form is bone meal, which is slow-acting and long lasting. Spread on your alpine bed in early spring at the approximate rate of a handful to the square yard (0.8 m²), it should keep the plants in good health for the rest of the year, with a possible boost in midsummer to encourage the late flowerers. It is best to fork it in lightly, if only to discourage the birds from mistaking it for their breakfast cereal. An alternative to the summer dose could be a half-strength watering with one of the liquid fertilizers like Maxicrop, Bio or Phostrogen.

A SELECTION OF PLANTS

Within the confines of this book, there is not room to describe more than a fraction of the vast variety of alpines available. Those listed here are all easily grown and readily obtainable, many from garden centres, others from specialist alpine nurseries – or from friends of course. To widen your scope, visit these nurseries if you can or write for their catalogues. (For general advice on propagating alpines, see p. 57.)

Bulbs (with one exception) have been omitted, because on the whole they do not fit very well into planting schemes for raised beds. The reason is that the leaves must be left on the plant till they have withered, in order to do their essential job of feeding the bulbs for next season. The dying foliage looks unsightly and can actually harm more delicate plants underneath. However, some of the small crocuses, such as *Crocus chrysanthus* and *C. biflorus*, may be introduced with care, but not *C. tommasinianus*, whose prolific seeding habit can make it a real menace. Very dwarf daffodils might also find a place, *Narcissus bulbocodium* and *N. asturiensis*, for instance.

(* = plants also suitable for growing in sinks and troughs – see p. 42.)

Aethionema pulchellum (*A. grandiflorum*).   A sun-lover with low woody stems clothed in small steely blue leaves. In June come 6-inch (15 cm) stems topped by dense cones of soft pink flowers. Remove these when the blooms are over and you are left with a handsome little 4-inch (10 cm) evergreen bush. Happy growing on the flat or cascading from a wall. Easily raised from seed sown in spring and kept in a cold frame.

A. 'Warley Rose'.*   Similar to the last, but more compact and not quite so striking in its foliage. Very free-flowering in early spring. Cuttings root easily in pure silver sand. (see p. 15).

Alyssum saxatile (*Aurinia saxatilis*).   The flamboyant if sometimes overdone gold dust. The type plant has a mass of brassy yellow flowers in early spring. 'Citrinum' is just as vigorous and free-flowering, with much more acceptable flowers of primrose yellow (see p. 6); 'Dudley Neville' has as many blooms in a fascinating buffy-biscuit colour. All three can be increased by seed or cuttings.

Androsace lanuginosa.   A beautiful Himalayan which, planted on the edge of a raised bed, will descend in a curtain of silvery leaves. The inch-wide (2.5 cm) heads of pink crimson-eyed blooms appear first in August and will go on till autumn.

A. sarmentosa (*A. primuloides*).   Has inch-wide (2.5 cm) rosettes of greyish hairy leaves from which emerge clustered heads of bright pink flowers on 3-inch (7.5 cm) stems. As the blooms fade, strawberry-like runners emerge from the rosettes, which root where they touch the soil to form a close sward of foliage. There are a number of forms, of which the best known are 'Watkinsii' and 'Chumbyi'. All must have an open sunny position and perfect drainage. For propagation, lift and pot some of the runners which have already rooted.

Anemone magellanica.   An utterly reliable plant, forming a basal clump of dark divided leaves above which the 10 to 12-inch (25–30 cm) stems carry many large creamy flowers in early summer. Increase by seed or division in spring.

17

A. nemorosa. Our native wood anemone has many forms and variations. The fact that it is usually found in woods as a wildling does seem to make it sulk when grown in the open garden. 'Robinsoniana' has very large flowers of soft lavender blue; 'Vestal' is pure white with a little pom-pom cluster in the centre of each flower; 'Alba Plena' is fully double and of snowy whiteness.

Antennaria dioica 'Rosea'. A carpeter making a low mat of silvery grey leaves. The 3 to 4-inch (7.5–10 cm) stems bearing heads of pink flowers come in late spring and early summer. There are several other forms, all of them useful and easy. May be used as a miniature groundcover for dwarf bulbs. Propagate by division in spring.

Aquilegia. Most of the larger aquilegias are best grown in other parts of the garden, but *A. caerulea*, with handsome blue and white flowers, grows to only about 12 inches (30 cm). *A. einseleana* is about the same height, with dusky violet-blue flowers. There is a dwarf 10-inch (25 cm) form of *A. canadensis*, with striking blooms of crimson and gold. All can be grown from seed, but as a genus they hybridize, so you may not always get what you expect.

Arabis ferdinandi-coburgii 'Variegata'. An invaluable low-spreading carpeter whose close-packed leaves are gaily striped in silver and green. There is also a newer form with leaves of gold and green. Both give year-round colour and are excellent cover for dwarf crocuses and the like. The spikes of white flowers appear very early in the year, but are of less importance than the evergreen foliage. Increase by simple division.

Aubrieta. Probably the most widely grown of all alpines, making swathes of vivid colour in spring on banks and retaining walls. It is easily raised from seed, although the many named forms must be propagated by cuttings to remain true. All, whether seedlings or named forms, should be cut back ruthlessly to the central cluster of foliage as soon as the flowers have faded. This will ensure vigorous growth and flowering next spring and possibly a few out of season blooms in autumn. Some of the best named varieties are: 'Carnival', in deep purple, strong-growing and free-flowering; 'Gloriosa', soft rose-pink flowers; 'Bressingham Pink', with double flowers of deeper pink (see p. 64); 'Mrs Rodewald' and 'Vindictive', in deep crimson. 'Argentea Variegata' and 'Aurea Variegata' have silver and gold variegated leaves respectively and lavender flowers.

Aurinia saxatilis. See *Alyssum saxatile*.

Campanula cochlearifolia (*C. pusilla*). A little charmer which will thread its way through larger neighbours without doing them any harm. In July and August comes a succession of thimble-sized bells of clear sky-blue on 3-inch (7.5 cm) stems. There are several colour variations including a white and a double. Easily increased by transferring the thread-like running roots in spring.

C. garganica. Happiest and most appropriate planted in a retaining wall, against which it will radiate foot-long (30 cm) stems strung with abundant blue star-shaped flowers throughout the summer. A plant of sterling worth, increased by cuttings of young growth in spring.

C. portenschlagiana (*C. muralis*). A vigorous hearty plant of immense value, which is equally happy growing out of a wall (*muralis* means wall) or on the flat, in sun or partial shade. The mass of lavender bells are produced almost continuously from midsummer till autumn. Cuttings of the new young shoots root easily in spring or an established plant can be divided.

Cerastium tomentosum. Snow in summer. On no account introduce this plant into your raised bed. Handsome though it can be in the right place, with its grey leaves and white flowers, it will invade and throttle any lesser neighbours and is almost impossible to eradicate.

Chiastophyllum oppositifolium (*Cotyledon simplicifolia*). A most useful and accommodating plant which is equally happy in sun or shade and in almost any soil. The 3-inch (7.5 cm) fleshy leaves form a low spread and in summer each 5 to

Above: the wood anemone, *A. nemorosa*, left, flowers from late March to early May

'Aurea Variegata', right, a delightful gold-variegated form of the well known aubrieta

Below: the striking *Chiastophyllum oppositifolium* flowers in late spring and summer

6-inch (12.5–15 cm) stem carries three or four dangling catkins of yellow flowers. It is shown off best in a raised position. To increase, just pull off a ready-rooted piece and plant elsewhere.

Chrysanthemum haradjanii. See *Tanacetum densum* subsp. *amani*.

Cyclamen hederifolium (*C. neapolitanum*). By far the most reliable of the hardy cyclamen, with beautifully marbled leaves, no one plant repeating the foliage pattern of its neighbour. The first flowers, in pink or white, appear in September, followed by the new leaves which remain all winter and spring, withering away as summer approaches. You may find seedlings emerging in odd corners of the garden, which have been carried by ants attracted to the sticky sweetness covering the newly ripened seeds. Happiest shielded from the hottest sun.

Daphne retusa. Perhaps the ideal dwarf shrub for a raised bed of restricted size. It is slow-growing, evergreen with glossy deep green leaves, and in late spring carries many little bunched heads of heavily scented blooms, crimson in bud, opening to white. It grows as a compact rounded bush and is unlikely to be more than 2 feet (60 cm) high even after many years' growth. It is sad that it is not more often grown or offered.

Dianthus 'Arvernensis'. Will form a close carpet, no more than an inch or two (2.5–5 cm) high, of grey leaves; in summer comes a generous offering of small sweetly scented pink flowers. Planted on the edge of a raised bed, it will in time spill itself down the wall. It loves sun.

D. deltoides. Of loose, rather floppy habit, the maiden pink produces an abundance of small flowers of bright crimson. There are several forms: 'Wisley Variety', with bronzy-coloured leaves and dark flowers; 'Steriker', dark green leaves and flowers of vivid intensity; 'Alba', with rather tatty white blooms. All are easily raised from seed.

D. 'Pike's Pink'. Nearer to a garden pink, but dwarf enough to hob-nob with alpines. Makes a low sward of silvery grey leaves and during summer produces a succession of smallish double pink lightly scented blooms on 4-inch (10 cm) stems.

Diascia 'Ruby Field'. In early summer this stunning plant makes a forest of 10-inch (25 cm) stems, which are strung with flat-faced twin-spurred flowers of a most unusual colour – variously described as salmon-pink, old rose, terracotta-pink, tangerine-pink, none of which quite defines this unique shade. They are produced continuously right into the autumn; in a mild year, even into November. It strikes easily from cuttings. In a very cold winter it may be hit badly in some districts, so keep a few cuttings in a frame.

Dryas octopetala. Mountain avens. A good-tempered plant of trailing or carpeting habit, whose woody prostrate stems bear oval veined glossy leaves. It will spread to a couple of feet (60 cm) or more across in time and has snow-white anemone-like flowers, followed by attractive fluffy seed heads.

Erinus alpinus.* The wild plant has many tiny mauve flowers strung up erect 3 to 4-inch (7.5–10 cm) stems. The most usually grown forms are 'Mrs Boyle', with clear pink flowers, and 'Dr Hanaele', in carmine-red. There is also a form with clean white flowers. Though individual plants are short-lived – perhaps two or three years – all forms will sow themselves about quite freely without ever becoming a nuisance. The spread of the clustered leaves is no more than a few inches (see p. 58).

Erodium macradenum (*E. petraeum* subsp. *glandulosum*). A beautiful and long-lived plant which unfortunately suffers a multiplicity of names and no doubt will

Opposite: the fragrant flowers of *Daphne retusa*, above, are followed by round red fruits

Euryops acraeus, below, an evergreen shrub valuable for both its foliage and flowers (see p. 22)

until the botanists reach agreement; *E. petraeum* is an alternative name, but that again branches off into several subspecies. All are of much the same habit and requirements, the main variation being in the silveriness of the finely dissected leaves and to a lesser extent the flower colour. The blooms are ¾ inch (2 cm) across, basically white or pinkish, intricately criss-crossed with a fine network of crimson veins. The upper two petals each have an almost black blotch at their base. Flowering starts in May and goes on continuously until autumn. It loves sun and grows no more than 5 to 6 inches (12.5–15 cm) (see p. 62).

Euryops acraeus (*E. evansii* of gardens). One of the most useful and beautiful dwarf shrubs, forming a dense dome of narrow evergreen leaves of shining silvery white. During summer it provides a generous number of inch-wide (2.5 cm) golden daisy flowers. Given time, it will grow to a foot (30 cm) or so high, with a spread of nearly double that. Coming from high in the Drakensburg mountains of South Africa, it is indestructibly hardy (see p. 21).

Gentiana acaulis.* One of the completely lime-tolerant gentians and one of the loveliest. It forms a congested sward of glossy leaves and in May appear huge stemless sapphire trumpets, speckled and striped with emerald in their throats.

G. septemfida. Could well be called everyman's gentian, being dependable and permanent as well as beautiful. It retires to ground level over winter, then makes semi-trailing stems during spring and summer, each one terminating in a cluster of five or six blue trumpet flowers in July and August. Completely lime-tolerant and can be raised from the plentifully set seed.

G. sino-ornata. Only for those gardeners with an acid lime-free soil. With these conditions, the summer growth of narrow leaves will be hidden under a solid canopy of glorious azure trumpets during September and October. There is a host of named hybrids from this spectacular plant, all needing the same soil conditions. Most can be increased in spring by division of the self-rooting sideshoots.

Geranium dalmaticum. A vigorous plant, quite without fads, quickly forming wide pads of rounded glossy leaves. In late spring and early summer the whole plant is smothered in clear pink flowers on 3 to 4-inch (7.5–10 cm) stems. Planted on the edge of a stone-built bed, the questing roots will find their way through the crevices and clothe an area of vertical wall.

G. 'Ballerina'. Forms concise clumps of ash-grey leaves and has a summer succession of inch-wide (2.5 cm) blooms of pink with a fine network of crimson veins. A distinct and beautiful hybrid growing no more than 8 inches (20 cm) high.

G. cinereum subsp. **subcaulescens.** The low mounds of greyish green leaves are hidden for several summer weeks by flowers of shattering crimson-magenta. Pays vivid dividends in any sunny well drained soil.

Globularia cordifolia.* Another plant which will gradually spill itself over the edge of a raised bed or trough, though equally happy spreading its carpet of dark glossy leaves on the flat. The flowers are like miniature mauve powder puffs, carried on 2-inch (5 cm) stems in June and July.

Gypsophila repens 'Dorothy Teacher'.* Will form a close bluish grey curtain of leaves and smother itself in a myriad of tiny pink flowers in May and June. Let it trail over the edge of a raised bed or trough (see p. 62).

Hacquetia epipactis. The little tight golden balls of flowers, each in the centre of a frill of apple-green bracts, appear newly minted in earliest spring, followed by the tripartite leaves which remain till autumn. It is happiest in a shady home and is easily raised from fresh seed (see p. 25).

Hebe 'Boughton Dome'. Forms an intricate dome of close packed stems clothed in tiny scale-like leaves of soft olive green, doing its best to look like a dwarf conifer. Never spoilt by flowers but gives a nice evergreen permanence to any planting scheme (see p. 59).

H. 'Carl Teschner'. Makes a network of woody stems clad in smally glossy leaves and in summer has innumerable 2-inch (5 cm) tapered spikes of lavender-blue

Above: most of the alpine geraniums, including G. *dalmaticum*, are easily grown in a sunny open situation

Gentiana sino-ornata proves irresistible to many gardeners but will only succeed in lime-free soil

flowers. With an overall height of 6 inches (15 cm), it will spread to a foot (30 cm) or more.

Helianthemum.   The so-called rock roses are nearly all forms or hybrids of *H. nummularium* and come in a variety of colours and leaf shades. They are rabid sun-lovers, invaluable for their ability to cover a lot of space in a short time and to give colour for many weeks in the summer. They are best cut back severely as soon as the flowers have faded to encourage new compact growth. All are good, but some of the better ones are: 'Amy Baring', dwarfer than most, only 3 to 4 inches (7.5–10 cm), with flowers which would match a free-range egg yolk; 'Cerise Queen', ill named for one with flowers of soft crimson; 'Fire Dragon', whose grey leaves contrast nicely with glowing orange blooms; 'Rose of Leeswood', double flowers of clear pink with grey leaves; 'The Bride', of virginal whiteness; 'Wisley Primrose', grey leaves contrasting well with primrose-yellow flowers.

Hypericum olympicum.   A most striking plant, which carries for most of the summer large flowers of rich gold whose centres are filled with a fuzz of yellow stamens. It grows as a compact bushlet of greyish leaves and will enjoy all the sun it can get.

Iris histrioides 'Major'.   A unique bulb, whose brilliant kingfisher-blue golden crested blooms appear in February and are quite impervious to whatever weather it may be asked to survive at that time of year. The flowers, which stand only 3 inches (7.5 cm) high and the same across, appear before the leaves, which will eventually lengthen to a foot (30 cm) or so but can be removed as soon as their work is done in early summer.

Leontopodium alpinum.   The edelweiss, about which so many absurd legends have been invented. In fact, given a sunny well drained soil, it is a perfectly easy, reliable and long-lived plant, producing its curious star-shaped flowers of off-white felt in late spring. It looks miserably dead during winter with no sign of life among the withered brown leaves, but is soon improved when the spring flush of new growth appears.

Lewisia.   Three or four closely related species of *Lewisia* have been hybridized over the years, by both man and bee, to give the race of plants now generally known as *L. cotyledon* hybrids.* Most alpine nurseries have their own particular strains, which are available in a wide range of colours – pink, red, flame, orange, yellow and white. The Sunset strain is the most vivid and varied. The blooms are usually striped and are borne in loose heads on 6 to 8-inch (15–20 cm) stems. The narrow fleshy leaves form flat rosettes up to about 6 inches (15 cm) across. Few other lewisias are dependable outdoors without special protection, but the cotyledon hybrids will flourish if planted on their sides in a wall, preferably not facing south. Seed is freely set and provides an easy means of increase.

Linaria alpina.*   A charming little denizen of high alpine screes, with narrow glaucous-blue leaves on prostrate stems and a long succession of small mauve eggy-lipped snapdragon flowers. Not long-lived as a rule, but scatters its seed about in a helpful way.

Lithodora oleifolium* (*Lithospermum oleifolium*).   A very dwarf shrub of gently running habit, making slender woody stems of 4 to 5 inches (10–12 cm) clad in handsome oval silvery grey leaves. The little pendant sky-blue flowers start arriving in early summer and continue for several weeks. The plant likes a well drained limy soil in full sun. It is also suitable for the alpine house (see p. 62).

Lychnis alpina.*   Forms neat tufts of narrow leaves and carries its clustered heads of pink flowers on 4 to 5-inch (10–12 cm) stems in spring. Easily raised from seed.

Omphalodes luciliae.*   The tufts of elegant spoon-shaped blue-grey leaves are a perfect foil for the large china-blue forget-me-not flowers, borne on trailing stems throughout the summer months. A great beauty which enjoys basking in full sun in a soil with plenty of lime.

Above: *Hacquetia epipactis* grows no more than a few inches high (see p. 22)

Below: flowering in spring, the *Lewisia cotyledon* hybrids like to be planted in a wall or rock crevice

Oxalis adenophylla. Some members of the genus should be avoided at all costs because of their dangerously prolific breeding habits. Not so this one, which makes concise clumps of curiously pleated grey leaves, with the pink funnel-shaped flowers nestling just above them in summer. The dried bulbs which are often available can sometimes be difficult to restart into growth, so it is wiser to shell out a few extra pennies and buy a pot-grown plant with roots.

Papaver alpinum.* Like a miniaturized Iceland poppy, with neat little mounds of finely dissected grey leaves and a succession of flowers in pale orange, soft yellow or white. Individual plants are short-lived but will self sow quite freely when happy.

Penstemon newberryi f. **humilior** (*P. roezlii* of gardens). The naming of penstemons is chaotic and the name "*P. roezlii*" is often used for this plant, though the true *P. roezlii* is seldom seen. Plants offered as *P. menziesii*, *P. newberryi* or *P. rupicola* may be so similar that it makes little difference, except that "*P. roezlii*" is usually the brightest coloured. Whichever you get, you will have a compact evergreen shrublet, no more than 4 or 5 inches (10–12.5 cm) high, with a spread of perhaps a foot (30 cm), which will display a mass of tubular flowers of rosy pink or bright crimson towards the end of May or early in June.

Phlox. There are many dwarf phloxes of varying forms and habits, most of which are easy long-lived plants and can be relied on to give a profusion of different colours in late spring. The creeping ones fall into two main groups, which are derived respectively from *P. subulata* and *P. douglasii*, though others may have had a hand in their parentage. As a rule, the subulatas are the stronger growers, expanding in time to 2 feet (60 cm) across but no more than 4 to 6 inches (10–15 cm) high, while the douglasiis tend to be dwarfer and more compact, with an ultimate spread of a foot (30 cm) or so and growing only a couple of inches (5 cm) high even when in flower. Both smother their carpets of small needle-like foliage with a solid mass of blooms in almost every colour except yellow or orange. Among the best subulata cultivars are: 'Daniel's Cushion', with large flowers of deep rich pink; 'Benita', with lavender flowers; 'G. F. Wilson', raised many years ago but still vigorous, with blooms of softest blue with small dark eyes; 'Red Wings', with large crimson flowers. Among the douglasii cultivars you cannot go wrong with: 'Crackerjack',* making a solid sheet of crimson, or 'Boothman's Variety', which is so generous with its dark-eyed lavender blooms; 'Lilac Queen'* is more compact than most and gives a canopy of deep lavender (see p. 39); 'Iceberg'* comes in palest ice blue and 'May Snow'* in purest white. There are many other named forms in both groups, all worthy of a place in your raised bed or paving, either as carpeters or trailers.

P. 'Chattahoochee'. An outstanding plant of loose habit, with foot-high (30 cm) stems clad in narrow leaves. The heads of long-lasting flowers start in May and continue for many weeks. Their colour is a unique glowing lavender-blue, each bloom centred with an eye of diffused crimson. It enjoys a well nourished soil in partial shade and is best trimmed to the ground when the flowers have at last faded (see p. 13).

Polygonum vacciniifolium. Planted where it can trail over a rock or wall, this plant will form a curtain of small glossy leaves and in September produce a forest of 6-inch (15 cm) stems closely packed with tiny pink flowers looking like little candles. They last well and, after the first sharp frost, prolong the display by turning to rusty red, when the foliage also colours well.

Primula. This is another vast genus of enormous diversity which it would be absurd to try and cover within the confines of this book; so I shall mention just a few from the group of the dwarf clump-formers, mostly forms and hybrids of *P. auricula*, *P. rubra* and *P. marginata*. They all make clusters of leaves and prefer a soil which does not dry out too easily (dig in some extra peat before planting) and a position shaded from the hottest sun. Most begin flowering in April. After a few

Above: *Papaver alpinum* is found wild in the European Alps

Below: *Penstemon newberryi* f. *humilior*, an outstanding plant for a raised bed

Pulsatilla vulgaris is easily increased from the plentiful seed, sown fresh in summer

years of happy growth, they can be lifted after flowering, split into several pieces and replanted.

P. auricula.*   The wild species can be a good garden plant, with several yellow flowers on each 3-inch (7.5 cm) stem, the new leaves attractively dusted with a creamy powder known as farina.

P. "belluensis".*   Of unknown origin and sometimes called *P.* 'Freedom', an appropriate name, for the lavender-coloured flowers are given with prodigious generosity. It will last many years undisturbed when happy.

P. 'Christine'.*   A compact grower and free flowerer with white-eyed blooms of glowing pink. Flowers a week or two later than most.

P. 'Faldonside'.   Dwarf and compact, with many blooms of dusky crimson.

P. 'Harlow Car'.   A strong grower with large flowers of warm creamy white held aloft on 4 to 5-inch (10–12.5 cm) stems.

P. 'Mrs Wilson'.*   Raised in the early years of this century, this is still one of the favourites, submerging its leaves under the ample heads of white-eyed purple flowers. It grows a mere 3 to 4 inches (7.5–10 cm) high.

P. marginata.*   A plant of variable flower colour in the wild and with many named forms. All are good, with lovely deckle-edged leaves dusted with creamy farina and flowers in any variant of mauve or lavender. It enjoys growing in a crevice.

P. 'Stuart Boothman'.   As hearty and original as the nurseryman whose name it bears. Compact heads of deep crimson blooms generously borne on 3-inch (7.5 cm) stems.

Pterocephalus parnassi (*Scabiosa pterocephalus*).   Makes a carpet of crimped greyish leaves and in summer has many little scabious-like lavender-pink flowers on short stems, followed by attractive fluffy seed heads. Enjoys life best in a sunny area with good drainage.

Pulsatilla vulgaris.   Our native pasque flower of chalky downlands. An established plant will produce a dozen or more large blooms of deep rich purple, their beauty enhanced by a central boss of golden stamens. They are carried on 6 to 8-inch (15–20 cm) stems which lengthen to a foot (30 cm) or so to carry the distinctive spiky seed heads. There are forms with red, pink, lavender and white flowers. All can be raised from seed, which must be sown as soon as ripe.

Ramonda myconi (*R. pyrenaica*). A plant which must have shade, preferably a shady crevice, where it will become a flat rosette of crinkly spoon-shaped leaves and bear many inch-wide (2.5 cm) blooms of lavender-blue, each centred with an orange beak of anthers. In very dry weather the leaves may curl inwards and feel flabby. Provided they are not left too long in this state, a good soaking will soon make them plump up and uncurl (see p. 13).

Salix alpina *(*S. myrsinites* var. *jacquiniana*). There are a number of very dwarf willows, most of them true alpines, which are charming plants for raised beds or troughs. This one makes a huddle of semi-prostrate woody stems no more than 6 inches (15 cm) high. Just before the small glossy leaves appear in spring, the stems are wreathed in petite ruby-red catkins.

S. serpyllifolia. Forms a network of absolutely prostrate woody stems which will follow the exact contour of any obstruction in its path. The tiny leaves are bright glossy green and appear at about the same time as the little yellow catkins.

Sanguinaria canadensis 'Flore Pleno' ('Multiplex'). Double-flowered blood root. The buds of this rare and beautiful plant arise from the fleshy roots, enfolded in the grey leaves, to emerge as many-petalled little snowballs of immaculate whiteness. It is partial to some shade, though it will grow in sun in a soil which does not dry out too quickly (see p. 30).

Saxifraga. A large and diverse genus with innumerable species and hybrids to gladden the hearts of alpine enthusiasts. For practical garden purposes, only three of the many groups into which they are divided botanically will concern us here. The Kabschias or cushion saxifrages are slow growers, forming tight buns of tiny close-packed leaves of grey, green or silver; they flower mostly in March and April in all shades of pink, yellow, crimson and white. The so-called silvers or encrusted saxifrages are well named, for their clusters of narrow leaves are pitted with limy exudations to give a silver effect. They flower in May or June, usually with white or creamy white blooms carried on sprays 4 to 6 inches (10–15 cm) long and up to a foot (30 cm) or more in some forms. They are natural crevice plants and display themselves better planted in a vertical wall or wedged between two rocks. The mossy saxifrages are usually stronger growers, making large rounded cushions of soft green foliage with blooms of white, pink or crimson on stems of about 6 inches (15 cm). I will mention just a few of the more vigorous ones in each group.

Kabschia group. *S. apiculata** has fresh green rosettes and four or five small flowers of sulphur-yellow on each 3-inch (7.5 cm) stem. S. 'Boston Spa' has fresh golden flowers. S. 'Bridget'* makes neat silver buns with several small pink flowers carried on maroon-coloured stems. S. *burseriana* 'Gloria'* has silver-grey foliage and large snow-white blooms in great profusion carried on crimson stems. S. 'Jenkinsae',* with tightly packed grey leaves hidden under a cloud of clear rose-pink flowers, is one of the very best.

Silver group. S. 'Burnatii'* has narrow intensely silver inch-long (2.5 cm) leaves forming a tight cluster and 6 to 8-inch (15–20 cm) closely packed sprays of purest white S. *callosa* (S. *lingulata*) is one of the parents of the last, with larger rosettes and longer looser sprays of white (see p. 34). S. *cochlearis* 'Major' has smaller leaves more densely packed and upright sprays of white blooms carried on red stems. S. 'Esther' makes a flatter mat of grey leaves with flowers which open pale yellow.

Mossy group. S. 'Cloth of Gold' has dense domes of bright gold leaves giving vivid year-round colour; the white flowers are of less importance than the foliage. S. 'Hi-Ace' is of similar size and habit, but the leaves are green, speckled with white, to produce an unusual frosty appearance; flowers white. S. 'Peter Pan' has bright green foliage and many pink blooms in early summer.

Above: *Sanguinaria canadensis* 'Flore Pleno' produces its lovely double blooms in spring (see p. 29)

(see p. 29)

Below: the variegated form of *Sedum kamtschaticum*, a handsome representative of this large and reliable genus

Scabiosa columbaria 'Nana'. A charming little scabious which, even in the poorest soil, will give a summer-long succession of lilac button blooms on 3-inch (7.5 cm) stems.

S. pterocephalus. See *Pterocephalus parnassi*.

Sedum cauticola.* One of the most attractive of a large genus. The winter resting buds grow from ground level during spring and summer to 6 inches (15 cm) or so, clothed in round fleshy leaves of dove-grey. In September and October they terminate in 2 to 3-inch (5–7.5 cm) flat heads of rich red flowers.

S. kamtschaticum 'Variegatum'. A long-season plant as gay as its name is hideous. All spring and summer the fleshy green leaves are boldly edged in gold; in late summer and autumn comes a generous supply of flat heads of flowers in crimson and gold.

S. spathulifolium 'Purpureum'.* In any dry sunny spot this plant will spread its carpet of small succulent rosettes coloured rich plum-purple. The 3-inch (7.5 cm) heads of yellow flowers appear in summer. In the form 'Cape Blanco',* often wrongly called "Cappa Blanca", the leaves are silvery grey. The two complement each other well.

S. 'Ruby Glow'. Of the same habit as *S. cauticola*, which was doubtless one of its parents, but larger in all its parts, the leaves flushed with red and the flowers ruby-red. It grows to 9 to 10 inches (23–25 cm).

S. 'Vera Jameson'. A stunning plant which makes arching 10 to 12-inch (25–30 cm) stems, bearing rounded fleshy leaves of rich purple all summer and with flat heads of dusky pink flowers in autumn. It is particularly effective growing beside any of the silver-leaved plants. The new shoots of this and the last root easily when about an inch (2.5 cm) long in spring.

Sempervivum. Houseleek. Another very large genus containing many species and numberless forms and hybrids. They will all survive with a minimum of moisture and nourishment, though repaying better conditions by more rapid growth. They have neat rosettes of fleshy leaves and enjoy unlimited sun. The flowers may be pinkish or off-white, but are of less significance than the decorative foliage which comes in a range of different colours. Three good ones which are usually available are: *S. arachnoideum*,* the cobweb houseleek, with a web of fine white hairs running from leaf-tip to leaf-tip; *S.* 'Jubilee', with larger rosettes in crimson and green; and *S. calcareum*, with rosettes which may be up to 6 inches (15 cm) across of a rich plummy red.

Silene schafta. A useful and easily grown late bloomer which produces a mass of rosy flowers from August on, in almost any soil or situation. A mature plant may be 18 inches (45 cm) across by about 6 inches (15 cm) high (see p. 61).

Tanacetum densum subsp. **amani** (*Chrysanthemum haradjanii* of gardens). A really excellent strong plant spreading into wide mats of silvery white leaves, individually doing their best to imitate a finely crafted ostrich feather. Give it sun on the edge of a raised bed and it will soon grow into a silver carpet of delight in spring, summer and autumn. The few yellow flowers are hardly worth mentioning; it is essentially a foliage plant.

T. herderi. Produces much the same effect as the last, but in a slightly more restrained way. The flat heads of summer flowers are long-lasting and quite acceptable.

Thymus × citriodorus. 'Silver Queen' and 'Aureus' make little low spreading bushlets whose variegated leaves in silver and gold respectively are deliciously lemon scented. 'Bertram Anderson' has leaves of solid gold, particularly vivid in winter.

Tiarella cordifolia. A shade-lover with pale green vine-shaped leaves and many tapered spires of creamy flowers on 9-inch (23 cm) stems. It spreads by runners which root like a strawberry and can be lifted ready-rooted and replanted straight away.

A native of Europe, *Veronica prostrata* is a sun-loving plant

T. wherryi. Not dissimilar to the last, but clump-forming and the flower spikes are pink-tipped. If given deep shade, it will flower continuously from May till September. No runners are made, but seed is set plentifully and should be sown as soon as it is ripe.

Tunica saxifraga. A charming sun-lover, like a miniature gypsophila, which develops into a summer cloud of myriad tiny pink flowers. A form, 'Rosette', has little flowers of snow-white which are fully double. Both like to hang down a wall face.

Veronica prostrata (*V. rupestris*). A showy and satisfying plant which produces a long summer succession of 6-inch (15 cm) spires of deep blue flowers. There is a pink-flowered form, 'Mrs Holt'; let them mingle together.

Sinks and troughs

The craftsmen who hewed out stone feeding and drinking troughs a hundred and more years ago could scarcely have guessed that they were leaving such a valuable legacy for the future. But that is the case. Like pieces of antique furniture, these old artefacts have acquired over the years a patina of their own – of moss, lichen and general weathering – and have become the cherished receptacles in which present-day gardeners grow their choicest alpine plants. Unfortunately, they have two drawbacks: their relative scarcity and their high price, the one induced by the other. Even the humble old stone kitchen sink, which can be used as a container for a rock garden in miniature, has become a collector's item.

GLAZED SINKS

There are alternatives, however. White glazed sinks, which are now being replaced in the home by plastic or stainless steel ones, can still sometimes be found in builders yards and bought for comparatively little. They are unthinkable as plant containers in their white nakedness, but they can be made quite acceptable by coating them with an easily made mixture known as hypertufa.

First wash and clean the sink and let it get dry. Then paint it all over the outside, 3 inches (7.5 cm) down the inside and round the corners for a few inches on the underside with the proprietary adhesive Unibond, using an ordinary paint brush. While this is drying, which may take an hour or two or most of the day depending on the ambient temperature, the hypertufa can be prepared. It should consist of equal parts by volume of sharp sand or fine grit, moss peat (not the darker coloured sedge peat) and cement. Make sure the three ingredients are well mixed before adding water, little by little, until you have a puddingy mix, which should retain its shape when a handful is squeezed. With too much water, it will slither off the vertical sides of your sink; with too little, it will not adhere properly before it hardens.

Once the Unibond is dry, or very nearly so, the hypertufa can be plastered on to the sink with your hands or with a trowel, in a layer about half an inch (1 cm) thick. There is no need to cover the whole of the inside, but it is best to take it 3 inches (7.5 cm) or so down the inside walls, so that none of the glazing will show when the sink is filled with soil. Similarly, the mixture should be

Saxifraga callosa 'Superba' cascading over the side of a trough (see
p. 29)

continued for a few inches round the base; this is made easier if
the sink is stood on a slightly smaller box. Once the work is complete, leave it for several days where air can circulate and your
newborn sink will then be ready to move into its permanent
position.

The peat in the hypertufa tends to hold moisture, which will
encourage moss and lichen to grow after a year or so, giving a
natural weathered look. The process can be hastened by dowsing
the outside with manure water, milk or water in which rice has
been boiled. Its water-holding capacity might be thought to make
the hypertufa vulnerable to flaking in severe frost, but it seems
quite impervious, although it will chip off if accidentally knocked
with a metal barrow or lawnmower. If you feel inclined, you can
also tool the coating when it is half hardened with an old chisel or
other blunt instrument, to produce a more realistic look of stone.
This should not be overdone, though a little scraping away with a
coarse file is justified to remove hard angles or any inappropriate
smoothness. The genuine stone troughs, after all, were seldom
very smooth or regular.

SIMULATED TROUGHS

If you cannot obtain or afford a genuine old stone trough, you can cast your own with hypertufa, using the same mixture of three equal parts of coarse sand, peat and cement. You will need a mould, which may consist of wooden planks, bricks or two cardboard boxes, with an inner box to support the inside walls until the hypertufa is set. The main difficulty with cardboard boxes is to find two large enough; also the moisture will soak into the cardboard and soften it, necessitating a few bricks to hold up the outside. Wood is undoubtedly the best material, with the pieces screwed lightly together so that they can be removed when the hypertufa has hardened. It has the further advantage that, if you are intending to make several troughs of different sizes, you can cast the largest first and then cut down the wood for the smaller ones (see figure 4, p. 36).

Whatever type of mould you use, some form of permanent reinforcement is required, especially if the trough is to be more than, say, 2 feet (60 cm) long. Galvanized wire netting will serve, or iron rods from a scrap metal merchant, and should be put roughly in the centre of both base and walls before adding the hypertufa. Have by you three or four pieces of wood, 6 inches (15cm) long, to make drainage holes; an old broom handle, sawn into lengths, is ideal for the job. These should be placed upright in the base before work starts and the hypertufa ladled in around them. They can be taken out quite easily once the mixture has set. Drainage holes are vital to prevent the trough being converted into a bog garden in heavy rain.

Old kitchen sinks, whether of stone or glazed, have their holes ready made, of course. However, authentic stone troughs were designed to hold liquids and must have holes made. With softish sandstone or Cotswold stone, they can be chipped out with a cold chisel and hammer; with the harder limestone or granite, an electric drill may be needed.

SITING AND SUPPORT

So you have your trough, old or new. Now where to site it? Choose an open position away from the shade of buildings and the drips from overhanging trees. This could be on a paved area or at the edge of a path where this is wide enough. If the trough is to sit on a lawn, it should be surrounded with paving stones sunk flush with the grass to allow for mowing.

The trough needs to be raised above the ground on a plinth of brick or stone, otherwise not only may the vital drainage holes get blocked, but it will lose all impact and importance, becoming an

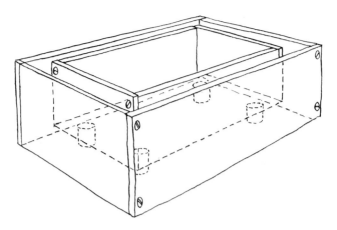

Figure 4: a wooden mould for casting a hypertufa trough

Figure 5: a brick plinth supporting a trough

object rather than a feature. The height of the plinth depends on the depth of the trough. According to the situation, it will usually look best with the upper edge of the trough 15 to 18 inches (38–45 cm) above the ground (see figure 5); more than 2 feet (60 cm) and it will appear top-heavy and off balance. It is vital to make sure that the trough is securely based on the support and cannot be dislodged by careless adults or the most obstreperous children.

SOIL AND ROCKS

With the trough firmly in position, preparation for planting can begin. First, put some large pieces of broken pot over the drainage holes, preferably three or four overlapping, so that water can escape but not the soil. Then, for a trough with an inside depth of 6 inches (15 cm) or more, spread a layer of coarse gravel or pot fragments over the whole of the base; it should be a couple of inches (5 cm) thick if the trough is only 6 inches (15 cm) deep, 3 to 4 inches (7.5–10 cm) if it is a foot (30 cm) or more deep. Next, an inch (2.5 cm) or so of very coarse peat or, if this is not available, half rotted leaf mould; its purpose is simply to prevent the finer soil, which goes in next, blocking the drainage holes.

For an average collection of dwarf alpines, a good standard soil mix would be four parts by volume of John Innes No. 2 potting compost to one part of coarse grit to ensure good drainage (see also p. 14.) Spread a few inches of this mixture all over the bottom of the trough, firm it well with your two clenched fists, put in a few more inches, firm again and repeat till you get to within an inch (2.5 cm) of the top. If the soil is not firmed, it will settle during the first few months and leave you with sunken plants surrounded by two inches (5 cm) of bare rim.

Rocks are the next thing to go in. These have a practical as well as aesthetic role, giving some of the plants a chance to find the coolness and extra moisture trapped beneath and between them. The ideal rock to use, if you can get it, is tufa – a very soft and extremely porous limestone formation, which is capable of absorbing a lot of water. It is so soft that inch-wide (2.5 cm) holes can be bored into it to provide perfect homes for young specimens of naturally cliff-dwelling plants, for instance, *Physoplexis*

Tufa provides a good home for the unusual *Physoplexis comosa* (see p. 46)

A trough with alpines planted between pieces of Welsh slate

comosa, *Potentilla nitida* or *Helichrysum milfordiae*. As bought from a garden centre or stone merchant, tufa is usually newly quarried and may look distressingly white and raw; but its water-holding capacity helps it to weather very quickly and in less than a year it will have toned down to an acceptable shade.

Failing tufa, try to find some other type of well weathered rock, the more rugged and knobbly the better. Take one fairly large piece and place it off centre in the trough, first having scraped out sufficient soil to bury up to a third of the rock. Firm the soil all round it with the handle of a trowel, then fit several smaller pieces round it, leaving crevices an inch (2.5 cm) or so wide between each rock. Make sure that each rock is firmly embedded in the soil. In a large trough you might have room for two outcrops, or an outcrop at one end with a selected single rock some way away to break up a large flat area. The aim should be to make each out-crop look as though it were originally one larger rock split up by frost and weathering, into which plants had established them-selves over the centuries.

PLANTING

Within the limited space of a trough, it is sensible to confine the choice of plants to those which are compact and slow-growing. This will allow for a wider range of shape and form and flower-ing times will be more varied. There are better places in the garden to grow such stalwarts as aubrieta, alyssum and the like. With a little care, twenty or more plants could be accommodated in a trough say 3 by 2 feet (90 × 60 cm). First, plant any crevices between the rocks, with such plants as silver saxifrages, very dwarf dianthus and compact sedums. Next, start on the open plains between the mountain ranges, choosing some of the low creeping plants like *Raoulia australis* and *Artemisia schmidtiana* 'Nana', interplanted with one or two upright growers such as *Allium cyaneum* to relieve the flatness. Arrange for a few trailing plants to drape themselves over the edge of the trough to break up the hard outline; *Gypsophila repens* 'Dorothy Teacher', *Globularia cordifolia* and any of the *Phlox douglasii* forms come to mind.

'Lilac Queen', one of the many *Phlox douglasii* cultivars which are ideal for tumbling over the edge of a trough (see p. 26)

Now to the tricky question of a dwarf conifer. Undoubtedly, this can give a wonderfully established evergreen effect to a well planned trough, but choose the wrong one and you can be in trouble. It might look very tempting as a small plant in a pot, but there are so many varieties with such varied rates of growth that it is vital not to select one which will swamp all its neighbours in a few years' time. The best course is to consult a knowledgeable nurseryman or a reliable book (for instance, the Wisley handbook on *Dwarf and slow-growing conifers*). The dwarf conifer most commonly seen in a trough is the Noah's Ark tree, *Juniperus communis* 'Compressa'; it is certainly one of the most attractive, making a dense little tapered upright column of blue-grey, and is so slow-growing that even after twenty years it is unlikely to have outgrown its allotted space. If you want a bun shape, one of the nicest is *Picea abies* 'Little Gem', a slow-growing globe of bright green needles.

With the plants all in, the last task is to cover the whole soil surface with grit or chippings. This is partly for cosmetic reasons, since it provides a more natural background for the plants, many of which come from very stony terrain. However, it also serves several practical purposes, by reducing evaporation from the soil, preventing the soil from caking and inhibiting moss from growing. In addition, it stops the low blooms from being splashed and it puts a barrier between woolly-leaved plants and the damp soil, which are otherwise prone to rot in excess contact with moisture. The ground flint sold as poultry grit is ideal, as it is a sympathetic grey colour and is itself impervious to moisture, but any stone chippings or pea gravel will do. Avoid too fine a grit, which may be disturbed by heavy rain or careless watering.

WATERING AND FEEDING

As isolated entities, troughs need particular attention in dry or very sunny weather, although like ordinary pot-grown plants, too much water can be as dangerous as too little. From October till about March normal rainfall should be sufficient, except in very unusual conditions. But during spring, summer and early autumn a careful watch must be kept. There are no hard and fast rules about exactly when to water; all you can do if in doubt is to scratch the soil surface and judge how dry it is. If it is just moist, delay watering for another day, then give it a really good soaking. In a prolonged drought, watering may be necessary every day, especially if the trough is shallow; a deeper one with a larger body of soil may hold out for several days. As a group, alpines generally prefer to be slightly under-watered rather than the opposite.

Above: *Dianthus alpinus*, a charming and colourful plant for a sunny situation (see p. 44)

Below: a corner of a trough with yellow *Alyssum serpyllifolium*, dark violet *Wahlenbergia (Edraianthus) serpyllifolia* and the unmistakable blue *Gentiana verna* 'Angulosa'

Aquilegia discolor bears its columbine flowers in May

Alpines in sinks and troughs do not require a lot of food. An early spring sprinkling of bone meal should keep them happy and floriferous without tempting them into excessive growth. Since many of them grow naturally in the poorest and stoniest of soils, they often flower more freely and retain their true character on a semi-starvation diet.

A SELECTION OF PLANTS

For further recommendations, see also the plants marked* in the list on pp. 17–32.

(** = plants also suitable for growing in an alpine house – see p. 52.)

Allium cyaneum.   Makes clusters of tiny narrow upright leaves among which in summer appear little bunches of pendant sky-blue flowers, the whole plant no more than 6 inches (15 cm) high.

Anacyclus depressus.**   The short prostrate stems carry much divided greyish leaves and in early summer a succession of daisy flowers, crimson in bud, opening in the sun to white, with a central disc of gold.

Androsace carnea.**   Forms 4-inch (10 cm) clusters of deep green leaves from which arise in spring 3-inch (7.5 cm) stems carrying many deep pink golden-eyed little flowers.

A. jacquemontii.**   From the Himalayas, this little charmer has intensely hairy half-inch (1 cm) rosettes from which emerge in May inch-high (2.5 cm) stems, each bearing a dozen or more blooms of deep pink. The plant increases by stolons which emerge from the rosettes soon after flowering, to root where they touch the soil.

A. sempervivoides.**   Similar in size and general habit to the last, but the leaves are deep green and virtually hairless so less vulnerable to winter damp.

A. villosa.**   Again about the same size and habit as the last two, but hairy-leaved. The flowers are white, each opening with a little central golden eye which turns crimson after a day or two.

Antennaria dioica 'Minima'.   A useful miniaturized ground-hugger for the open flat areas of a trough. The small grey leaves form a carpet barely half an inch (1 cm) high. The little clusters of everlasting flowers on 2-inch (5 cm) stems arrive in spring.

Aquilegia bertolonii.   A real delight, with large tubby blooms of deep uniform sapphire on stems not more than 3 to 4 inches (7.5–10 cm) high.

A. discolor.   Similar in size to the last, but the flowers are pale blue with white centres.

Armeria cespitosa.**   A very dwarf thrift making rounded domes of tightly packed rosettes, with many little balls of pink flowers sitting almost stemlessly on the foliage.

Artemisia schmidtiana 'Nana'.**   A beautiful trailer which, planted on the edge of a trough, will hang down in a curtain of finely cut silver foliage. The greyish flower spikes are of no importance and rather spoil the effect, so are best cut off as

The spring flowers of *Dryas octopetala* 'Minor' give way to feathery seed heads in summer (see p. 44)

they appear; it is essentially a foliage plant. It is sometimes hit in a really severe winter, but strikes easily from cuttings which will survive quite happily in a cold frame.

Campanula arvatica.   A gem of a plant, quite robust but so gentle that it can safely be allowed to wander around and through other plants without doing them any harm. Each thread-like 3-inch (7.5 cm) stem carries several star-shaped flowers of deep purple. There is also a beautiful snow-white form, 'Alba'.

Dianthus alpinus.   Creates tight clusters, seldom more than 4 inches (10 cm) across, of glossy bright green leaves which are hidden in late spring under a canopy of large speckle-centred blooms of rich pink on inch-high (2.5 cm) stems. There is also a remarkable form called 'Joan's Blood', with blooms of deep blood-red and almost black centres. Both set seed freely, but are likely to embrace the attentions of other nearby dianthus, so don't expect always to get true plants from seed. Cuttings root easily enough (see p. 41).

D. freynii.**   Of doubtful name but undoubted charm, forming dense pads of small silvery grey leaves and flowering freely with small pink blooms, each speckled with crimson in their centres.

Draba aizoides.   In earliest spring the clusters of bright yellow flowers on 2-inch (5 cm) stems appear above the clumps of bristly rosettes. A rare British native. Seed is set generously and often makes the plant self-generating.

D. bryoides var. **imbricata**.**   An enchanting plant which forms itself into a slowly expanding dome of minute tightly packed rosettes, turning to vivid emerald in early spring, and then produces a wealth of tiny golden flowers on 2-inch (5 cm) thread-like stems. It is the perfect plant to grow in a block of tufa.

Dryas octopetala 'Minor'.   An exact counterpart to *D. octopetala* (see p. 20), reduced in all its parts to half size, making it ideal for a trough. Planted near the edge, it will trail down and display its white flowers and fluffy seed heads (see p. 43).

Erodium reichardii** (*E. chamaedryoides*).   The congested clumps of small rounded leaves are an excellent foil for the succession of half-inch (1 cm) flowers in spring, summer and autumn. Their basic colour is pink or sometimes white, delicately criss-crossed with a network of crimson veins. As a native of Majorca, it may be spoiled by a particularly vicious winter, so keep a few cuttings in the safety of a cold frame. In the alpine house it will be much less vulnerable and will bloom for ten months of the year.

Gentiana verna 'Angulosa'.   Surely the epitome of all alpine plants, with its dazzlingly blue star-shaped flowers. Not a very long-lived plant as a rule, but supremely lovely while it lasts. Give it a soil which will not dry out during summer and more food than most alpines will tolerate – an extra pinch or two of bone meal or even a small dozzle of well rotted cow manure beneath its roots. Seed is plentifully set and can be raised with skill and patience.

Hebe buchananii 'Minor'.   An attractive miniature evergreen shrublet making a dense bun of wiry stems clothed in small scale-like leaves. It occasionally adds a few small white flowers as an afterthought.

Helichrysum milfordiae.**   A plant whose intensely hairy rosettes of silvery white need perfect drainage. It will get this if planted in a crevice between two lumps of tufa, where it will spread by rooting into the rock. With such a near-starvation diet, it usually flowers more freely, bearing inch-wide (2.5 cm) papery blooms, crimson in bud, opening to white, on 3-inch (7.5 cm) stems. When happy, it is a very beautiful plant. In the alpine house it will be scarcely affected by winter damp and, the poorer and grittier the soil, the better it will flower.

Linum salsoloides 'Nanum'.   A completely prostrate flax whose creeping wiry stems are clad in tiny needle-thin leaves. In summer the funnel-shaped flowers of pearly white appear for several weeks.

Above: *Erodium reichardii*, a relative of geranium, has been cultivated in Britain since the eighteenth century

Below: 'Angulosa', the most commonly grown form of the glorious spring gentian, *G. verna*

Oxalis enneaphylla.** From scaly underground roots come curious inch-wide (2.5 cm) circular leaves folded into pleats. The funnel-shaped blooms nestle snugly among these in early summer. There are several forms of this intriguing plant with pink or white flowers.

Penstemon hirsutus 'Pygmaeus'. A nice dwarf, with bronzy leaves and a long succession of heads of lavender-flushed tubular flowers in late spring and early summer.

Physoplexis comosa** (*Phyteuma comosum*). A plant of most unusual and compelling beauty. Small toothed leaves emerge in spring (excellent slug fodder, so take precautions) and in June the extraordinary flowers appear – clustered heads like a collection of tiny flasks, swollen at the base and tapering to a purple tip through which the almost black stigmas protrude. Outdoors it is best started as a young plant in a hole in tufa. Also a fine alpine house plant (see p. 37).

Potentilla nitida.** Another plant which grows very happily in tufa, where it will make a low carpet of silver leaves and produce a modest succession of stemless pink blooms from May onwards. The form 'Rubra' usually blooms more freely than the type plant.

Raoulia australis.** Its tiny leaves, barely $\frac{1}{8}$ inch (3 mm) long, cluster tightly together to form an absolutely flat carpet of brilliant silver. In summer there may be a scattering of flowers like small yellow pearls, but the spectacular foliage is the attraction. In a very cold or wet winter it may suffer, so pot up a few rooted pieces in autumn and keep them in a cold frame. It is worth it.

Saxifraga. Many of the slightly less vigorous members of the Kabschia group (see also p. 29) are perfect trough plants, slowly developing into tight little buns of close-packed grey or silvery leaves and smothering themselves in short-stemmed flowers in earliest spring. Among innumerable named forms seek out the following:** *S.* 'Arco-Valleyi', with silver-grey foliage and stemless pink flowers of gentle pink; *S. burseriana* 'Crenata', snow-white with petal edges quaintly crinkled, and 'Sulphurea', sulphur-yellow flowers on 2-inch (5 cm) crimson stems; *S. diapensioides*, with silver foliage and several clean white flowers on each stem, very slow-growing and excellent in tufa; *S.* 'Iris Prichard', with large blooms of an unusual apricot shade; *S.* 'Kellereri', small pink blooms on red stems, often starting to flower in January and continuing sporadically for the rest of the year; *S.* 'Lady Beatrix Stanley', deep pink, almost crimson flowers on very short stems and green foliage; *S.* 'Marie Louise', several snow-white flowers to each stem and very early flowering.

Silene keiskei 'Minor'. A Japanese species with narrow bronzy leaves on the 6-inch (15 cm) stems which are topped by a succession of clear pink flowers in July and August. Easily raised from seed.

Thalictrum kiusianum. Another Japanese whose tiny divided leaves look like a miniature maidenhair fern. The flowers appear in early summer on 3 to 4-inch (7.5–10 cm) thread-like stems and consist of little balls of mauvy pink stamens. A charmer which retires below ground for winter. The running roots can be divided in spring.

The alpine house

Basically, an alpine house serves two main purposes. First, it enables the relative newcomer to alpines to grow some plants in pots, where there is more control over any particular soil or watering needs of individual plants. With shelter from hostile weather outdoors, many plants will perform just that little bit better, especially those which put on their best display in early spring; broken or mud-spattered blooms will be avoided and they will, of course, flower a little earlier. When the weather cannot make up its mind if it is winter or spring, it is also comforting for the owner to be able to enjoy the plants at close quarters, in the relative shelter of even an unheated house.

Secondly, when the gardener has become thoroughly addicted to alpines and is more ambitious, an alpine house gives scope for experimentation with some of the plants which cannot normally be grown out of doors in that collection of weather samples we call a climate. Such plants as *Primula allionii*, dionysias and the high alpine androsaces come into this category. It is not the cold from which they require protection; overhead moisture is the chief enemy, particularly during the winter.

One of the many desirable forms of an alpine gem, *Primula allionii* (see p. 55)

VENTILATION

An alpine house is nothing more complicated than an ordinary unheated greenhouse with all the extra ventilation possible. Most greenhouse manufacturers these days can supply additional louvre-type ventilators for the walls and hinged ones for the roof. These should preferably be fitted into alternate rows of glass on both sides and in the roof. The idea is not to cosset the plants but to prevent rain from falling on them. Some of the cushion plants, in particular, resent being constantly sodden. From about May until the middle of September, all the ventilators can safely be left fully open. From September till things brighten up with some sunshine in spring, the side vents can be permanently shut, while the top ones can be kept open to allow air circulation and closed only when driving rain or snow might be blown in.

SHADING

Some form of shading is essential. Many of the cushion plants especially are vulnerable to scorching if the full force of summer sun through the glass is not moderated. The Netlon brand of shading is adequate, but tends to go brittle and tear after a couple of years' exposure. Rokolene netting is more satisfactory and is made in several different densities. The 40 per cent grade is best for alpines, breaking the full glare without causing the plants to be etiolated or drawn. It can either be stretched over wooden frames or attached to the wooden spars of the greenhouse with drawing pins. If the house is made of aluminium, the netting can be held in place with a few large bulldog paper clips clamped over it and on to the metal spars. Another alternative is the shading known as Coolglass, which is painted or sprayed on the outside of the glass. It is cheap, appears to last a full season and is easily removed in autumn. The shading, of whatever type, should normally go on about the middle or end of May and stay in position until mid-September.

SOIL

As with alpines grown outdoors, a well drained soil is important. An average mixture for alpines in pots would be equal parts by volume of John Innes No. 2 potting compost, moss peat and sharp grit or very coarse sand. For some of the choice and more demanding plants, the high alpine androsaces for instance, use more grit and less peat; primulas in the Auricula or Pubescens groups would be better given less grit and more peat. This may sound complicated, as if you have to know the exact requirements of every plant you grow; but the more one has to do with plants, the more one realizes how astonishingly adaptable they are. Soil is only one factor needed to help them flourish, and dogmatism has no place in the garden – on this or any other subject.

BENCHING

If possible, avoid slatted benching: it allows too much air to circulate round the pots and tends to make them dry out too quickly. Trays covered with an inch or two (2.5–5 cm) of stone chippings are much better. Best of all is to build a trough about 9 inches (23 cm) deep round three sides of the house and fill it with a mixture of coarse sand and fine gravel. The pots can be sunk up to their rims in this, saving an enormous amount of watering. In fact, for anyone who is away at work all day or perhaps away from his plants for several days at a time, such a plunge bed is almost essential. Many of the plants will start life in 3- or 4-inch (7.5–10 cm) pots and, standing in isolation, these will dry out very quickly in hot weather, especially if they are of clay. The plunge bed is most easily made with Dexion angle-iron, which can be cut

Figure 6: a plunge bed round three sides of an alpine house

to length and bolted together through the slots provided. This framework can then be lined with wooden planks treated with Cuprinol, leaving slight gaps or boring plenty of holes in the base to allow surplus water to drain away quickly. Make sure that the supporting legs are resting on a solid base, such as a whole brick or even a concrete block. Even in a small greenhouse of 8 by 10 feet (2.5 × 3 m), the bench when filled will weigh nearly 2 tons (see figure 6, p. 49).

WATERING

The question of clay or plastic pots is a vexed one. Most alpine plant enthusiasts still have an inbuilt dislike or mistrust of plastic pots, but apart from any aesthetic consideration, there is really very little validity in these feelings. Plastic pots do have certain advantages, the main one being their ability to hold moisture longer than clays, because there is no evaporation through the pot wall. However, precautions must be taken to ensure that this is not overdone and to prevent waterlogging. Any alpine grown in a plastic pot has to be given absolutely perfect drainage by the addition of extra grit to the soil mixture.

On the other hand, if the pots are to be buried up to their rims in a plunge bed, clay pots must be used, in order to benefit from the exchange of moisture which takes place between the soil in the pots and the surrounding sand and gravel. With this method, every pot is given a good soaking in late autumn and is unlikely to need any further watering until spring arrives, just an occasional soaking of the sand or gravel as it dries out. Once the warmer weather comes, it is simply a case of keeping the sand moist all the time and giving individual pots a good soaking if they dry out.

Free-standing pots, whether of clay or plastic, should be kept constantly moist during the growing season and watered just enough to prevent plants withering during the winter rest period.

Having potted your plants into appropriate soil and suitably sized pots, the final touch is to cover the soil surface with grit or chippings, preferably poultry grit, or a jig-saw of small flat rocks. As well as giving a more finished look, this has the same practical value as with a trough (see p. 40). In the case of pots, it also, of course, considerably reduces the amount of time spent watering.

FEEDING

With a reasonably good soil mixture, to which a modest pinch of bone meal has been added in the initial potting, it should not be necessary to feed in the first year of growth. After that, one or two half-strength feeds with one of the proprietary liquid plant foods or another pinch of bone meal, when growth starts in spring, should keep most alpines in good health and prevent both starvation and too vigorous growth. As the plants grow, they will need to go into larger pots, but it is a mistake to over-pot them. So many alpines are used to having their roots restricted in the confines of a narrow crevice that they will not suffer, as stronger plants might, from being slightly pot-bound. Many will actually enjoy it.

COLD FRAMES

For gardeners who cannot accommodate an alpine house but want to grow some of their alpines in pots, the alternative is a cold frame. This can be an ordinary wooden garden frame covered with a dutch light in winter; or people with a DIY bent can construct a frame very simply with concrete building blocks, using one at the front and two at the rear, which gives sufficient depth to grow most alpines and enough slope to shed the rain. The plants will be happiest, and need less frequent watering, if the pots are plunged to their rims in the fine gravel and coarse sand mixture suggested for an alpine house plunge bed (see p. 49). Shading in summer is easily provided by attaching 40 per cent Rokolene to the dutch lights with drawing pins, having spare lights with Rokolene but no glass for the plants which do not need protection from rain. The frame should be south-facing if possible, with a west aspect as second best.

The frame can also be raised 2 feet or so (60 cm) above ground on brick pillars or up-ended concrete paving slabs, with the base made of paving slabs set $\frac{1}{4}$ inch (0.5 cm) apart to allow water to drain away freely. This has the merit of bringing plants and host into more intimate contact, to the advantage of both. It also of course saves a lot of stooping if that is not your favourite position. It is a type of frame which has been used by some of the most successful amateur growers of alpine plants and has produced excellent results.

A SELECTION OF PLANTS

There are no hard and fast rules as to which plants can or should be grown in an alpine house; it must be the choice of the individual. The following are just a few of the more suitable plants, together with those marked ** in the list on pp. 42–46.

*** = plants which must have protection in most parts of the country, or at least, are likely to give a better account of themselves.

Androsace cylindrica.* Forms a tight little dome of close-packed grey rosettes, which is hidden in early spring under the thousands of white yellow-eyed blooms. Keep water off the leaves, particularly in winter, and give it an extra collar of chips to sit on.

Campanula 'Joe Elliott'. A hybrid (raised by me) between *C. morettiana* and *C. raineri*. In a gritty limy soil it will go on producing its shallow bell-shaped lavender-blue flowers from early summer till late autumn. It grows no more than 5 to 6 inches (12.5–15 cm) high. It can also be grown in a sunny well drained trough or in a hole bored into a tufa block. Increase by cuttings in spring or by division.

C. morettiana.* A beautiful inhabitant of limestone cliffs in the Dolomites, needing special care and devotion in a very gritty soil. The tiny hairy leaves are very susceptible to excess moisture. Each short trailing stem carries an upright-facing bell of lavender-blue, which should be removed as soon as it fades. There is a very lovely pure white form, 'Alba'.

C. zoysii. A unique beauty whose little half-inch (1 cm) tubular blue bell flowers are puckered together at their mouth. The tiny round leaves are bright glossy green. It can be grown in tufa outdoors provided slugs can be kept at bay.

Convolvulus boissieri* (*C. nitidus*). The carpets of inch-long (2.5 cm) leaves look as if they were fashioned from beaten silver. Stemless white funnel-shaped flowers grace the plant in summer.

Dionysia aretioides.* By far the most amenable of a genus known to be extremely challenging. Also one of the most beautiful. In a nice gritty soil it will form a loosely domed cushion of soft grey-green rosettes, the whole of which is hidden under a canopy of yellow primrose-scented blooms in April.

Helichrysum coralloides. A shrublet of great originality and distinction. The scale-like leaves fold themselves flat against the little branches to give a snakeskin effect of silver and green. Very slow-growing, it may eventually attain a height and width of 8 to 10 inches (20–25 cm).

Lewisia. While some of the lewisias can be grown outdoors if given just the right conditions (see p. 24), most are safer in the alpine house where they are usually perfectly dependable and very floriferous. Apart from *L. cotyledon* in its many forms, look out for *L. columbiana* ssp. *rupicola*** (often offered under the name 'Rosea' — a gross misnomer for the flowers are near magenta); the leaves are narrow and almost tube-like and the rosettes only 2 to 3 inches (5–7.5 cm) across. *L. tweedyi*** is the most sumptuous gem of the genus, with short-stemmed blooms 2 inches (5 cm) across, of crystalline texture, in slightly varying shades of apricot. But it needs rather special treatment, with a minimum of water after flowering in May, kept normally moist during August and September, after which it should be kept almost bone dry until the following early March (see p. 54). Most of the other species can be watered normally from March till October, then kept very much on the dry side in winter.

Lithodora oleifolium. See p. 24.

Above: *Campanula* 'Joe Elliott' is equally happy in a sunny trough or in an alpine house

Below: a native of Iran, *Dionysia aretioides* was introduced in 1959

Ranunculus calandrinioides flowering in the open in January

Opposite: a pale form of *Lewisia tweedyi*, one of the most challenging members of the genus (see p. 52)

Primula.   Any of the many named forms of *P. auricula*, *P. pubescens* and *P. marginata* (see p. 26) are excellent pot plants for the alpine house. Give them a little extra peat in their soil and keep them out of the full glare of the sun and they will reward you with a colourful spectacle in April and May.

P. allionii.***   A jewel of a plant found wild inhabiting a few limestone cliffs on the French-Italian border of the Maritime Alps. It clings to the cliff faces, making domes of close-packed rosettes of sticky greyish leaves and producing many stemless primrose flowers in a wide variety of shades of pink. This variation in colour has given rise to numerous named forms raised from seed, of which there must now be over 40 to choose from, all worthwhile (see p. 47). It is a plant which needs special loving care in cultivation. It can only be grown in an alpine house or cold frame in this country and the tightly packed leaves are highly vulnerable to the grey mould fungus. Give it a particularly well drained limy soil with a good collar of grit round its neck, water meticulously round the leaves, never on them, and the reward will be great as the flowers start opening in February or March. It is important to remove the flowers as soon as they fade, to prevent them rotting. As well as a wide range of colours from pink and red to almost crimson and white, the flowering times of the different forms vary widely. 'Praecox' will often produce a flower or two before Christmas, with others following till mid- or even late April. Other good forms to look for are: 'Anna Griffith', with cut-petalled blooms of palest pink; 'Avalanche', in clear white; 'Crowsley', in deep plummy crimson; 'Snowflake', with large white flowers; and 'William Earle', in rich purplish crimson.

Ranunculus calandrinioides.   A plant which produces its 6-inch (15 cm) grey wavy-edged leaves in late summer, then in any mild spell in winter or early spring will bear large white or pink buttercups. By early summer it has retired below ground again.

Soldanella alpina should be protected from winter wet and slugs

Saxifraga. All members of the Kabschia group (see p. 29 and 46) make fine alpine house plants. Also several from the other groups, notably *S. retusa*, looking like a petite carpet of moss with each little inch-high (2.5 cm) stem carrying a compact head of crimson flowers in May. And most particularly *S. grisebachii* 'Wisley', with wonderful symmetrically arranged leaves forming inch-wide (2.5 cm) rosettes of silver. In the very early days of the year the centre of each rosette turns crimson and grows out into what looks like a huge angry caterpillar of crimson bracts. It is a unique and sensational plant.

Soldanella alpina. From among the small kidney-shaped leaves of deep green, the 4-inch (10 cm) flower stems rise early in the year, each carrying two or three deeply fringed pendant bells of amethyst-blue. A real enchantress.

Propagation

The equipment needed for the propagation of alpines is simple, consisting of no more than a cold frame. A small plastic propagator with undersoil heating will speed up the process of germination with seeds and of root formation with cuttings, but it is a luxury rather than a necessity.

SEED

Peat-based seed compost is not recommended for alpine seeds. It is intended essentially for short-term plants, which will go out into the garden within a month or two, whereas many alpine plants will remain in the same pots for a year or more after sowing and some may be there for a year before they even germinate. John Innes seed compost with some added grit is a far more suitable medium.

When to sow is a vexed question. Seeds of certain plants must be sown as soon as they ripen – pulsatillas, cyclamen, and most gentians, for instance. Others can safely be left for sowing in February or March. If in doubt, a general rule is to sow the seed soon after it is ripe, which, after all, is what nature does. Seed which is to be sown in spring should be stored in an unheated shed, not in a heated house.

Fill the pot with the compost to within an inch (2.5 cm) or so of the rim, firm with the finger tips, then level it gently with the base of another pot and lightly dust the surface with compost through a fine kitchen sieve. Sow the seeds at a wide spacing and then sieve a minimum of compost over them. Finally, put a thin layer of fine grit on top, just enough to hide the soil. This will help conserve moisture, stop the soil caking and also inhibit the formation of moss and liverwort, which might choke the young seedlings.

If possible, the pots should be plunged to their rims in sand in the cold frame, which will save a lot of watering. They must be kept permanently moist. Frost will not harm them; in fact, it will hasten germination in some cases.

CUTTINGS

This is an alternative means of propagation, and it is the only one for named hybrids and forms if they are to remain true to their originals. Many alpines can be easily increased by 1-inch (2.5 cm)

Hebe 'Boughton Dome', an excellent dwarf shrub for a raised bed (see p. 22)

Opposite: *Erinus alpinus* 'Mrs Boyle' self-sown in a Cotswold wall (see p. 20)

long cuttings of soft young growth in spring. Put them in pure silver sand and keep in a shaded cold frame, never letting the pots get dry and maintaining a moist atmosphere in the frame. Such plants as the creeping phloxes, *Campanula garganica*, *C. portenschlagiana* and the dwarf penstemons can all be treated like this. Helianthemums, which make their most suitable soft growth after flowering, can be dealt with in the same way during summer, kept in the frame all winter and potted in spring. Cuttings of woodier plants, such as dryas, euryops, globularias and hebes, are best taken when spring is past and put into a rooting medium of equal parts of peat and silver sand or perlite.

DIVISION

Simple division involves digging a plant up, gently pulling it into several pieces and either potting the divisions to get them established or often replanting them straight away, ready-rooted. This method can safely be used with many of the primulas, immediately after flowering, and with *Geranium dalmaticum*, *Arabis ferdinandi-coburgii* 'Variegata' and others. Some of the more fragile plants like *Campanula cochlearifolia* are better established in pots before going into their new homes.

Pests and diseases

PESTS

Like most plants, alpines can sometimes be attacked by garden pests such as aphids, caterpillars, slugs and snails, though on the whole they are much less subject to such evils. For aphids, the best remedy is one of the systemic insecticides, for instance, dimethoate or pirimicarb. These are absorbed into the body of the plant, so that the pests are poisoned as they suck the sap, and one application will keep the plants immune from renewed attacks for several weeks. Caterpillars may occasionally damage both leaves and flowers; derris powder, HCH or permethrin is effective. Slug pellets can be used against slugs and snails.

One of the most insidious pests is vine weevil. The plump white maggots with brown heads, barely half an inch (1 cm) long and curled in a half circle, live just below the soil surface and have a voracious appetite for plant roots. The first sign of their presence is when the plant looks withered, by which time it is probably too late to save it. After pupation, the grubs hatch into small dark brown beetles, which hide during the day and feed on the leaves and flowers at night. The adults lay many eggs in spring and summer. Vine weevil will attack almost any plants, but among alpines, primulas, sedums and saxifrages are particular favourites. If you should be unlucky enough to be troubled with these little brutes, dust all your beds with HCH, or apply it in liquid form, and from then on mix HCH powder into the soil for anything to be grown in pots.

The only serious fungal problem suffered by alpines is grey mould, *Botrytis cinerea*. This causes rotting of the leaves, stems and flowers, which become covered in grey-brown mould. Good hygiene and ventilation are the best means of prevention and control. Remove any dead flowers promptly, keep the alpine house well ventilated and avoid damp or shaded situations outdoors. At the first sign of the disease, remove affected parts of the plant and burn them to stop further infection. Fumigate the house with tecnazene smokes, or spray plants with captan, carbendazim, benomyl or thiophanate-methyl.

The undemanding Silene schafta can contribute late summer colour to a raised bed (see p. 31)

Above: *Gypsophila repens* 'Dorothy Teacher', left, a useful trailer for the edge of a raised bed or trough (see p. 22)

Erodium macradenum, right, from the Pyrenees, flowers from May until August (see p. 20)

Below: *Lithodora oleifolium* requires perfect drainage and full sun (see p. 24)

Further Reading

Collins' Guide to Alpines, Anna N. Griffith. Collins, 1973.
Manual of Alpine Plants, Will Ingwersen. Cassell, 1978, 1991.
The Propagation of Alpines, L. D. Hills. Faber, 1959.
Alpines in Sinks and Troughs, Joe Elliott. Alpine Garden Society, 1974.
Alpines in Pots, Roy Elliott. Alpine Garden Society, 1970.
Propagation of Alpine Plants, J. K. Hulme. Alpine Garden Society, 1969.
Alpines, Lionel Bacon. David & Charles, 1973.
Alpines in colour, Will Ingwersen. Blandford, 1981, 1991.

A raised bed of unusual shape at Threave Garden in Scotland

The double-flowered *Aubrieta* 'Bressingham Pink' (see p. 18)